ALASKA

Sarah Tieck

Big Buddy BOOKS
Explore the United States

VISIT US AT
www.abdopublishing.com

Published by ABDO Publishing Company, PO Box 398166, Minneapolis, MN 55439.

Printed in the United States of America, North Mankato, Minnesota.
022012
092012

 PRINTED ON RECYCLED PAPER

Coordinating Series Editor: Rochelle Baltzer
Contributing Editors: BreAnn Rumsch, Marcia Zappa
Graphic Design: Adam Craven
Cover Photograph: *Shutterstock*: R. Peterkin.
Interior Photographs/Illustrations: *Alamy*: Daniel Tycholiz (p. 27); *AP Photo*: Fairbanks Daily News-Miner, John Wagner (p. 26), Charles Gorry (p. 13), Al Grillo (p. 21), Stephan Savoia (p. 25), Klas Stolpe (p. 19); *Getty Images*: Jimmy Johnson/The Image Bank (p. 17), Hank Ry/Time Life Pictures (p. 23); *iStockphoto*: ©iStockphoto.com/bradwieland (p. 30), ©iStockphoto.com/brytta (p. 27), ©iStockphoto.com/DmitryND (p. 30), ©iStockphoto.com/mchebby (p. 27), ©iStockphoto.com/PaulTessier (p. 5), ©iStockphoto.com/toddmedia (p. 9), ©iStockphoto.com/yenwen (p. 11); *Shutterstock*: Walter S. Becker (p. 29), M. Cornelius (p. 30), Sam Dcruz (p. 9), Scott Kapich (p. 26), Phillip Lange (p. 30), oksana.perkins (p. 19).

All population figures taken from the 2010 US census.

Library of Congress Cataloging-in-Publication Data

Tieck, Sarah, 1976-
  Alaska / Sarah Tieck.
      p. cm. -- (Explore the United States)
  ISBN 978-1-61783-340-3
  1. Alaska--Juvenile literature. I. Title.
  F904.3.T54 2012
  979.8--dc23
                              2012000752

ALASKA

Contents

ONE NATION

The United States is a **diverse** country. It has farmland, cities, coasts, and mountains. Its people come from many different backgrounds. And, its history covers more than 200 years.

Today, the country includes 50 states. Alaska is one of these states. Let's learn more about Alaska and its story!

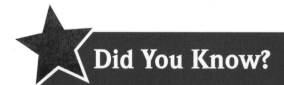

Did You Know?

Alaska became a state on January 3, 1959. It was the forty-ninth state to join the nation.

Mount McKinley (*above*) is one of Alaska's famous places.

ALASKA UP CLOSE

The United States has four main **regions**. Alaska is in the West.

Alaska has no states on its borders. The Arctic Ocean is north. The Bering Sea is west. The Gulf of Alaska and Pacific Ocean are south. And, the country of Canada is east.

Alaska is the largest state. Its total area is 590,693 square miles (1,529,888 sq km). About 700,000 people live there.

Did You Know?

Washington DC is the US capital city. Puerto Rico is a US commonwealth. This means it is governed by its own people.

6

REGIONS OF THE UNITED STATES

Legend:
- = West
- = Midwest
- = South
- = Northeast

CANADA

WASHINGTON
MONTANA
NORTH DAKOTA
MINNESOTA
VERMONT
MAINE
NEW HAMPSHIRE
OREGON
IDAHO
WYOMING
SOUTH DAKOTA
WISCONSIN
MICHIGAN
NEW YORK
MASSACHUSETTS
RHODE ISLAND
CONNECTICUT
PENNSYLVANIA
NEW JERSEY
NEVADA
UTAH
COLORADO
NEBRASKA
IOWA
ILLINOIS
INDIANA
OHIO
Washington DC ★
WEST VIRGINIA
DELAWARE
MARYLAND
VIRGINIA
PACIFIC OCEAN
CALIFORNIA
KANSAS
MISSOURI
KENTUCKY
NORTH CAROLINA
ATLANTIC OCEAN
ARIZONA
NEW MEXICO
OKLAHOMA
ARKANSAS
TENNESSEE
SOUTH CAROLINA
MISSISSIPPI
GEORGIA
TEXAS
LOUISIANA
ALABAMA
FLORIDA

ARCTIC OCEAN
BERING SEA
ALASKA
CANADA
GULF OF ALASKA
PACIFIC OCEAN

MEXICO
HAWAII
GULF OF MEXICO
PUERTO RICO

N
W E
S

IMPORTANT CITIES

Alaska's **capital** is Juneau (JOO-noh). It is the state's third-largest city, with 31,275 people. This city is located in southern Alaska.

Juneau is surrounded by water, mountains, and forests. People cannot drive cars to get there. They have to fly in on airplanes or ride in on boats!

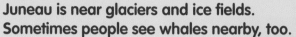

Juneau is near glaciers and ice fields. Sometimes people see whales nearby, too.

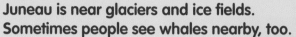

Juneau became Alaska's capital in 1906. The state capitol building (*below*) is located there.

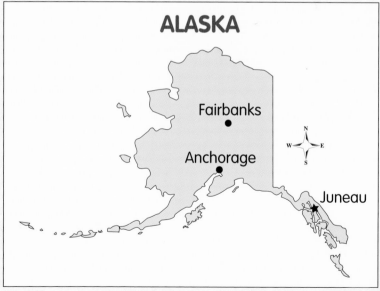

ALASKA

Fairbanks

Anchorage

Juneau

N
W · E
S

Anchorage (ANG-kuh-rihj) is the largest city in Alaska. It is home to 291,826 people. Oil, railroads, and military bases are important to this growing city.

Alaska's second-largest city is Fairbanks. It has 31,535 people. Fairbanks is close to the Arctic Circle. The Arctic Circle is far north, so it gets very cold there.

Anchorage is a modern city with a strong business community.

11

ALASKA IN HISTORY

Alaska's history includes native Arctic tribes and **frontier** life. Inuit (IH-noo-wuht), Aleut (a-lee-OOT), and other tribes have lived in Alaska for many years. People from Russia explored and settled the land in the 1700s. Many were fur traders.

In 1867, the US government bought Alaska from Russia. Many Americans thought this land only had snow. They said it was a waste of US money! But, others knew it had important natural **resources**. Alaska became a territory in 1912 and a state in 1959.

In 1959, President Dwight D. Eisenhower signed papers to help make Alaska a state. Alaska became the first new state in almost 47 years!

Timeline

1867

The US government bought Alaska from Russia for $7.2 million. This was about two cents per acre!

1896

A gold rush began in Alaska and a part of Canada called the Klondike.

1800s

1884

The US Congress established laws, federal courts, and public schools in Alaska.

Juneau became Alaska's **capital**.

1906

1989

The *Exxon Valdez* oil tanker lost 11 million gallons (42 million L) of oil in the Gulf of Alaska. This was one of the largest oil spills in US history.

1959

Alaska became a state on January 3.

1912

Alaska became a US territory.

2011

Lawmakers argued about drilling for oil in Alaska.

1900s

2000s

An earthquake happened near Anchorage and Valdez on March 27. It was one of the largest known earthquakes in North America.

1964

Alaskan Sarah Palin was John McCain's **running mate** in the 2008 presidential election. They lost to Barack Obama and Joe Biden.

2008

15

ACROSS THE LAND

Alaska has mountains, oceans, **glaciers**, and forests. It has many wildlife **refuges** and a lot of open land. Some parts of Alaska are above the Arctic Circle.

Many types of animals make their homes in Alaska. Some of these include moose, polar bears, caribou, and grouse. Many fish live in Alaska's rivers and off its coasts.

Did You Know?

Since Alaska is so large, temperatures are different throughout the state. Average summer temperatures range from 35° to 75°F (2° to 24°C). In the winter, the averages range from -20° to 40°F (-29° to 4°C).

★★★★★★★★★★★★★★★★★★★★★★★★★★★★★★★★★★★

Alaska is home to some of the largest wildlife refuges. The Arctic National Wildlife Refuge is one of them. Many animals, such as caribou (*above*), live there.

17

EARNING A LIVING

Alaska is known for its rich natural **resources**. These include fish and oil. **Commercial** fishing provides many jobs. Oil creates important businesses, too.

Tourism is also a major business in Alaska. The state is a popular vacation spot. So, many Alaskans work in jobs that help visitors.

Did You Know?

Captain Vitus Bering arrived in Alaska in 1741. Years later, the Bering Sea was named for this explorer from Denmark. Today, commercial fishermen work in the Bering Sea.

Cruises have become popular vacations in Alaska.

Catching salmon and other fish is often dangerous work!

19

SPORTS PAGE

When people think of Alaska, many think of sled dogs. That's because the state is home to the Iditarod Trail Sled Dog Race.

This famous race starts every year on the first Saturday in March. It covers about 1,100 miles (1,770 km) from Anchorage to Nome. In 2002, Martin Buser broke a record when he finished in just under nine days!

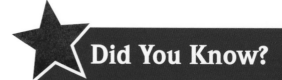

Did You Know?

People have used sled dogs for more than 1,000 years. Native Americans used sled dogs instead of horses to pull things.

People who command sled dogs are called mushers. Each Iditarod musher works with 12 to 16 dogs.

HOMETOWN HEROES

Many famous people have lived in Alaska. Edward Lewis "Bob" Bartlett is famous for helping Alaska become a state.

Bartlett was raised in Fairbanks. He worked as a gold miner and a newspaper reporter.

In 1945, Bartlett began representing the Alaska Territory in the US Congress. He talked to lawmakers about making Alaska a state. In 1959, Bartlett became one of Alaska's first US senators.

Bartlett helped pass many new laws. Buildings, hospitals, and schools in Alaska are named for him.

23

Sarah Palin is another famous Alaskan. Palin grew up in Skagway. She worked as a sports reporter and a mayor. In 2006, she became Alaska's governor.

In 2008, Senator John McCain ran for president with Palin as his **running mate**. They lost. But, Palin became famous. She was the second woman to run for vice president from a major political party!

When Palin became famous, many people learned more about Alaska.

Tour Book

Do you want to go to Alaska? If you visit the state, here are some places to go and things to do!

 **See**

The highest mountain peak in North America is Mount McKinley. It is 20,320 feet (6,194 m) tall.

 Cheer

Watch the Iron Dog snowmobile race. It is about 2,000 miles (3,220 km) long! The race starts near Wasilla. Racers stop for a halfway break in Nome. The race ends in Fairbanks.

 ## ★ Explore

Wrangell-Saint Elias National Park and Preserve is the largest US park and preserve. Glaciers and mountains cover its land. Grizzly and brown bears, caribou, wolves, and sheep live in the park.

★ Learn

Alaska is home to many totem poles. These were made by Native Americans. They are most common in southeastern Alaska and western Canada.

★ Discover

Go for a drive on the Alaska Highway. It is 1,523 miles (2,451 km) long. It runs from Fairbanks to Dawson Creek in British Columbia, Canada.

A Great State

The story of Alaska is important to the United States. The people and places that make up this state offer something special to the country. Together with all the states, Alaska helps make the United States great.

★ ★

Alaska is a state filled with natural beauty. The northern lights are sometimes seen in Alaska's night sky.

Fast Facts

Date of Statehood:
January 3, 1959

Population (rank):
710,231
(47th most-populated state)

Total Area (rank):
590,693 square miles
(largest state)

Motto:
"North to the Future"

Nickname:
The Last Frontier

State Capital:
Juneau

Flag:

Flower: Alpine Forget-Me-Not

Postal Abbreviation:
AK

Tree: Sitka Spruce

Bird: Willow Ptarmigan

Important Words

capital a city where government leaders meet.
commercial (kuh-MUHR-shuhl) meant to make money.
diverse made up of things that are different from each other.
frontier the edge of settled land, where unsettled land begins.
glacier (GLAY-shuhr) a huge chunk of ice and snow on land.
refuge a place that provides shelter or protection.
region a large part of a country that is different from other parts.
resource a supply of something useful or valued.
running mate someone running for vice president with another person running for president in an election.
tourism the business of providing hotels, food, and activities for travelers.

Web Sites

To learn more about Alaska, visit ABDO Publishing Company online. Web sites about Alaska are featured on our Book Links page. These links are routinely monitored and updated to provide the most current information available.

www.abdopublishing.com

Index